तेजोमय ग्रन्थ माला

Right Thinking

Swami Tejomayananda

Central Chinmaya Mission Trust

•

First Printed in United State of America - 10,000 copies
Reprint in India upto 2007 - 26,500 copies
Revised Reprint - November 2009 to January 2010 - 7,000 copies
Revised Edition - February 2013 - 3,000 copies

•

Published by:
Central Chinmaya Mission Trust
Sandeepany Sadhanalaya, Saki Vihar Road,
Mumbai 400072, India
Tel.: +91-22-2857 2367, 2857 5806 Fax: +91-22-2857 3065
Email: ccmtpublications@chinmayamission.com
Website: www.chinmayamission.com

•

Distribution Centre in USA:
Chinmaya Mission West
Publications Division
560 Bridgetown Pike, Langhorne, PA 19053, USA
Tel.: (215) 396-0390 Fax: (215) 396-9710
Email: publications@chinmayamission.org
Website: www.chinmayapublications.org

•

Designed by:
Chinmaya Kalpanam, Mumbai

•

Printed by:
Usha Multigraphs,Pvt. Ltd Mumbai-13 Tel.: 0222 4953546

•

Price: ₹ 45/-

•

ISBN 978-81-7597-554-5

CONTENTS

Preface

Our true nature is pure happiness. This is what the philosophy of Vedānta declares. This realisation is veiled by many false notions about ourselves and the world. It keeps us searching for happiness and peace where they do not exist. Right thinking alone can remove this veil of ignorance and allow us to enter into the inner sanctorum of joy which is our own nature.

In three delightful talks, Pūjya Gurujī Swami Tejomayananda points out, with both seriousness and humour, what is wrong thinking and how it can be corrected. Right thinking, Pūjya Gurujī says, transforms our entire personality. One can discover true success, peace, joy, and freedom within one's own being. The highest vision of absolute Oneness, which is the culmination of all education and knowledge too gets revealed through right thinking. Thereafter, one lives a perpetually inspired existence, loving, serving and spreading joy to all beings around.

In short, right thinking leads us to the Truth – the Truth that sets us free.

Brni. Arpita

Education and Knowledge

The words information, education and knowledge, apart from their dictionary meaning, have a general meaning as understood by people and also a special meaning indicated in the scriptures. I will start with what is generally understood and then I shall try to explain its significance from the spiritual standpoint.

Education and Knowledge

We understand the word education to mean knowledge imparted in schools and colleges where students study various subjects. Learning of the 3 R's (reading, writing and arithmetic) is understood as basic education. After school, they choose a professional course, to study more and more in that particular area. For this, we send them to educational institutions with special facilities and say, "We are sending them for higher education; we are giving

1

them the best education". We do not say we are giving them the best 'knowledge', but that we are giving them best 'education'.

Education that is given in schools and colleges is usually the collection of data, whereas knowledge is the discovery of Truth. We can teach a child to read and write, but we cannot give him knowledge or insight into the true nature of a thing. We may attempt to give him data, but he will have to realise it within, for himself. For instance, we can teach a child grammar, but we cannot impart to him a comprehensive understanding of the language itself. Many of us know what nouns and adjectives are; yet use them incorrectly in sentences. On the other hand, some of the greatest poets have not even had a formal education, yet their compositions are faultless and immortal.

What can we understand from this? Education is a collection of information, which can be imparted or conveyed to a person. Knowledge is something that must be discovered. Knowledge gets revealed by contemplating upon a thing and tuning our mind to it.

Though many graduate with honors in science, how many become scientists who make discoveries? Discoverers are very few. Similarly, real artists are also very few. I too, have learned biology and physics, but I remember nothing of the subjects. All I recall about them is that they were the subjects I studied in school! Chemistry, physics and biology – I can use the names, but I have not understood what they are, or why I learned them. It is only by the grace of God that I passed my exams. I got a degree, but that degree did not give me knowledge.

When we use our sense organs to collect information or our intellect to analyse a thing, we get partial knowledge; and at times without any real understanding. A specialist too knows more and more about less and less. A patient went to an ENT doctor with a right ear ache. The doctor referred him to another specialist, claiming to be only a left ear expert! Knowledge is whole. Education, which leads to a path of discovery and complete knowledge alone has truly served its purpose.

Setting a Higher Goal for Life

Education only gets us a degree which many a times may get us a good job. It is usually job-oriented. On completion of university education, the graduate is conferred with a certificate with no guarantee even of a job. After getting a degree, if we are unable to find a job we get frustrated. If we could get a good job without a degree, many would have no interest in education. Our educational system prepares us only for one aspect of life, but it does not prepare us to live life completely.

The typical student today does not think about the goal of life. He merely thinks about achieving a professional or material goal like becoming a doctor and earn a lot of money. Many times he has no guidance and no ideal to follow. The duty of the educational institution is to provide guidance and also to prepare the student for life. It must show him higher goals that he can strive for. We all know that when we set for ourselves a higher goal, we strive hard to attain it even though we may not actually be able to reach it. But when there is no ideal, we do not work and there is no progress or development.

For example, if we decide to feed others before feeding ourselves, then we will strive to do that. Otherwise we will only think of feeding ourselves and eat without feeding another. If our ideal is baser then we would not only eat our own food but the food of others as well. We notice that when our ideal falls, so does our behavior.

For many, the knowledge they acquire is merely kept in their heads and never applied; and for some, it remains in the book – the book that is locked in a library with the key in the pocket of the librarian who has gone on a holiday! So their knowledge is also on a holiday! There are people who are walking encyclopedias or talking libraries, but with no real knowledge or understanding. Someone once said to Pūjya Gurudev Swami Chinmayananda, "I have gone through the *Bhagavad Gītā* several times but nothing has happened". Pūjya Gurudev replied, "You have gone through the *Bhagavad Gītā*, but has the *Bhagavad Gītā* gone through you?" The purpose of education is to impart knowledge by which we can discover the truth for ourselves and to train us to see life in its totality and face it with all the consequences of our actions.

Purpose of Knowledge: Inner Transformation

Education should bring about an inner transformation in a person. There should be a positive change, a blossoming of the personality. Such a transformation can happen only with the discovery of Truth. Knowledge of the Truth transforms a person, but mere information does not. It is sad that in spite of so much education, our lives have not changed. We are still the same.

Ādi Śaṅkarācārya states the purpose of knowledge precisely – 'vidyā phalam syāt asato nivṛttiḥ – The result of knowledge is the elimination of falsehood'. This implies that if I have understood something as false, I withdraw from it. When the wrong concept has gone, wrong conduct also comes to an end. Right knowledge transforms our thinking and actions. We may have based our lives upon certain concepts, but once we realise they are wrong we should let them go and not hold on to the false notions.

Removal of False Concepts

Once, as a man was walking down the road, he saw

a shining object. Thinking it to be a piece of silver, he stopped, looked around and as no one was looking, picked it and put it into his pocket. He was happy that he had found something precious. He went to a quiet place and took the object out of his pocket. He then realised how foolish he had been, for the shiny object was a stone wrapped in silver paper. He immediately threw it away. Would he then boast about his foolishness? He probably will never talk about the incident. Even if he does, it would only be to illustrate how he was tricked into wrong thinking by his sight and greed.

True knowledge gives humility. Partial knowledge may make one arrogant but deeper knowledge or wisdom alone brings humility. True knowledge brings an end to all our sufferings and we become totally different persons. Very often our education, rather than removing false concepts about life, only seems to strengthen them. Seekers of Truth should put forth all efforts to free themselves from all wrong concepts. We should wake up from our sleep of illusions.

What are these wrong concepts? There are many. The main one is that I think myself to be the physical body. When I talk about myself or introduce myself, I refer to my physical body as me. This is not true.

Another wrong concept is that money can give me security. Without money, I am insecure. However, this is fallacious. It is seen that even a billionaire may feel insecure and a pauper feel monetarily secure. Sometimes it is seen that the more the money, the more the fear one seems to have. So can money be a source of true security?

Another false concept is that more the comforts and objects of pleasures I possess, the happier I will be. A person who has lots of money can buy many pleasures and must therefore be very happy. But is the wealthy man always happy? Are not many suffering in luxury and comfort?

Happy Man's Shirt

There once was a king who felt very sick. He called many doctors. All said that there was nothing wrong with the king physically and that they could not help him feel healthy. A wise man who came to see the king told him that if he was to wear the shirt of a happy man, his illness would vanish, and he would become well again. The king instructed his minister to bring to him the shirt of a happy man. Everyone was surprised at this, for they thought that the king himself must be the happiest man, since he had so many priceless shirts!

The minister looked all over the land. He asked a rich businessman, who replied, "But who told you I am happy? I am envious of my neighbour as he is richer than me. Go to him". So the minister asked the neighbour who said, "I am not really happy. I have no children. What is the use of all this wealth?"

And so the search for a happy man continued. Then finally one day, the minister saw a man sitting on the banks of a river, looking very peaceful and happy. He asked him, "Are you happy?" He replied, "Doubtlessly so!" The minister asked, "Will you give me your shirt?" He replied, "Shirt? What shirt? I have never worn one!"

The minister then explained that their king was sick and was told that by wearing the shirt of a happy man he would become well again. This great Master told him to tell the king that happiness and sorrow come only from within. When we know this, we will not seek outer objects (shirt) in order to be happy. We will then seek the true source of happiness which is within ourselves.

We are troubled by our erroneous notions – that I am the body, that money gives me security and that pleasures will make me a happy person. Unfortunately man is usually respected only for his wealth, power and possessions rather than for what he is. If he does not possess much money nobody seems to care for him. A person should be respected for what he 'is' rather than what he 'has'.

Highest Knowledge: The Vision of Oneness

One of the meanings of knowledge (jñāna) is vision. The *Bhagavad Gītā* classifies vision as noble (sāttvika), ordinary (rājasika), and ignoble (tāmasika).

Noble Vision (sāttvika jñāna): We perceive this world with the duality of the Seer and seen. No two things in the world that we perceive through our senses or conceive through our mind and intellect are the same. Everything is different from the other.

To see differences is the function of our gross and subtle equipments. But while we perceive difference, the understanding by which we are able to recognise the oneness in manyness is called a noble vision. To see the unity in diversity is a noble vision. To see the one Reality that pervades all the differences is the highest knowledge.

Our physical body is a good example of this. The hands, the head and the legs all are different but in my understanding I know that all are me. The 'I' vision pervades all different limbs of my body. If somebody touches my back, I say, "Why are you touching me?" The best vision, then, is to be able to see the one Reality that pervades all the names and forms of the Universe.

Ordinary Vision (rājasika jñāna): When the perceived differences alone are considered real, it is a rājasika vision. We then give importance only to differences and understand each thing to be separate and unconnected to others. The world then is not seen as a whole, but is considered as parts, unrelated to each other. The objects of the world are categorised as 'my' as opposed to 'not my'. That is why we fight over my house, my share, your share and so on. Though the Lord has created only one earth and space, we have divided it into nations with even national 'air spaces'! This is rājasika jñāna or a divisive vision.

Ignoble Vision (tāmasika jñāna): With this vision one mistakes the part for the whole and gets very attached to that part – be it an object, a person, an opinion or a belief. For example, the feeling that 'my path alone is right, yours is wrong', 'my religion alone is good, yours is not', 'my God alone saves, yours can not' and so on. The person with such a vision can become intolerant and fanatical. For one who thinks in a narrow and petty way, there are always conflicts.

Result of Oneness: Love and Service to All

We can learn a lot regarding the noble vision from our attitude towards our own body. I will not cut off the finger because it has hurt my eye accidently. In fact, the fingers will wipe the tears from the injured eye. Also if by mistake I bite my tongue, will I remove the teeth or punish them? No, because the teeth are also me, and is just as dear to me as every other part of the body. I have neither hatred towards any part, nor desire to give it pain. Where there is a sense of oneness there is love and when there is love there is a desire to serve.

Presently we are not able to serve others because there is no love and because we have no sense of oneness. Education must give us this noble vision. This will bring about transformation within and in the world. If one person changes, he can change the world around him. That one person can start a ripple effect. Saints and sages have a great influence on thousands of people. They hate none and are friendly with all.

When we say that the world is terrible, we must remember that being a part of the world, we are condemning ourselves. We too have contributed towards it. When we begin to change our vision of the world, there will be peace and goodness. A vision of absolute oneness is the highest knowledge. This is propagated by Vedānta – the philosophy of non-dualism (advaita).

Peace of Mind

I cannot give you peace of mind, but I can give you a piece of advice on the topic. This advice is not original – a new discovery. It is a time tested way. Generations of great people who practised and lived it have verified and confirmed its efficacy.

Peace always seems to elude us. We experience a little peace now and then in our lives. In deep sleep, when the mind is not functioning, we experience peace. This peace of 'no mind' is experienced by us only in deep sleep. Some therefore conclude that to be peaceful the mind must stop functioning. But can we attain such peace even while the mind is functioning?

Desires cause agitations in the mind. A desire-ridden mind is never at peace. When we are enjoying, the desire is being fulfilled, so there is a temporary cessation of desire and the mind feels peaceful. But once the enjoyment is over, the same desire or new and old desires crop up and we are agitated again. Such peace is indeed fleeting.

Between two wars there is a period of temporary peace. When a riot takes place in a city and the police curb it by force, there is an uneasy calm. This peace is fragile and may shatter in a moment's notice.

People with a religious inclination feel peaceful when they are praying in a temple, a mosque or a church. Some feel calm as they sing in praise of God and some when they listen to spiritual discourses. As long as one is praying, chanting or listening to discources, the peace remains. Thereafter again agitation starts.

Peace is Not Achieved by Struggling or Not Struggling

Why do we feel restless and agitated in the midst of changing circumstances? This is only because we are seeking, searching and striving desperately to attain peace. The more we look and struggle for peace, the more we are agitated. This is the paradox.

So will we find peace when we stop struggling or searching for peace? First of all can we give up struggling? Our attempts to give up the struggle will cause more frustration and agitation. Therefore, giving up the struggle is also no solution for gaining peace.

Vedānta says, '*aprayatnāt prayatnāt vā muḍho nāpnoti nivṛttim* – Neither by not struggling nor by struggling does man attain peace. He who knows the Truth attains it.' (*tattva niścaya mātreṇa prājño āpnoti nivṛttim*).

A man of action always thinks that a person sitting in a state of meditation is doing nothing. He is useless and unproductive – a mere idler. Although it may appear so, that person is at peace; which is not an easy accomplishment. His mind is calm and absorbed without being drugged or in a stupor. This peace is a dynamic quietude, an equipoise achieved without struggle. How, does a person gain such peace?

This peace cannot come from anything external. This is the basic fact we have to understand.

Peace is Our Nature

Our minds are usually restless and agitated. We

thrive on sensations from newspapers, novels or movies. Naturally, as we seek sensation, peace eludes us. We expect to gain peace by some external means, even as agitation gurgles within us all the time.

The scriptures say that we cannot get peace from outside. For example, in this hall if all of us stop talking, peace will be there. It is not outside. It is not created. In fact, we can only create disturbance. There was peace before the disturbance, it exists even during the disturbance and will become evident when the disturbance ends.

Ripples arise in the water. Before the ripples were created, the water existed. When the ripples are perceived the water exists and when the ripples subside, water remains. In the same way, peace is always present. We create disturbances – agitation, distraction and restlessness – and then we seem to 'lose' that peace.

A verse from the *Bhagavad Gītā*[1] beautifully explains who can attain lasting peace. 'He, who lives

---

[1] *vihāya kamān-yaḥ sarvān-pumaṁś-carati nispṛhaḥ,*
nirmamo nirahaṅkāraḥ sa śāntim-adhigacchati. (2.71)

in the world, giving up desires and cravings, is free from attachment and sense of 'I' and 'mine', attains peace'.

It is interesting to note that the *Gītā* does not say what we must do, but, rather, what we must get rid of to attain peace. What a wonderful thing – we are not told to do something, but are assured that peace is ours if we give up these four causes of agitation.

Sources of Disturbance

It is these four – desire, craving, 'I-ness' and 'my-ness' – that disturb us and destroy our peace. Superficially it would seem that the one who relinquishes these four would be stone-like. *Gītā* assures us that such a person is successful in the world. Therefore, we need to investigate what these four mean.

Desire: Can anyone really be free of desire? A person may desire to have a glass of water or he may express the desire to sleep. No one can be free of such simple desires. They are basic needs that must be satisfied. Hence, we should understand the difference between a desire and a basic need.

Different people desire different objects. Everyone seems to want something or the other. But on further inquiry we realise that no one really wants objects for their own sake. We are actually seeking something else from those objects.

What do we really want from objects? If we wanted objects, then when we get them, we should be happy and satisfied. But, we are not. We do not really want objects but we want joy or happiness through objects. So the real desire is to be happy. In fact, the attainment of happiness is the culmination of all of our struggles and searching. The problem is that we want happiness, but we strive to gain objects, mistakenly attributing happiness to them. The result is that our real desire is never fulfilled. We constantly change places, objects, relationships – everything, in order to gain happiness. Alas, we never change ourselves or our thinking.

Our physical life depends on physical things. To satisfy hunger, food is required. To protect us from cold, warm clothing is required. These are basic needs. Satisfying them may make us comfortable, but not happy. We are confused between happiness and comfort. Comfort does not necessarily bring happiness. Nowadays, our life has become more comfortable and we have become comfortably sorrowful! When *Gītā*, advises us to give up the desire for objects *(vihāya kamān yaḥ sarvān)* it means understanding fully that we are seeking happiness, not objects.

A wise person gives up the desire for objects, understanding fully well that what he seeks is true and lasting happiness, which he cannot get from objects. He understands that sorrow comes from a sense of incompleteness and not lack of objects. We usually think that sorrow will vanish if we get this thing or that. We think, 'With that person, I will be complete'. Then, when the relationship ends, we feel we cannot survive.

A wise person does not expect lasting happiness from objects. If the nature of objects was happiness, they would have universally brought happiness to everyone all the time. For example, the nature of sugar is sweetness. It is sweet for all, at all times. Objects or beings do not give happiness to all at all times. However, there is no need to throw away the objects. We need only to give up our false belief that they will bring lasting happiness. A wise person may even desire objects, but he will never insist on the fulfilment of such desires.

Happiness lies Within

If there is no happiness in the objects themselves, then what is the source of happiness? There are only two entities in this world of experience. One is 'I', the experiencer and the other is the world of objects. If happiness is not in the world of objects, what remains is the subject, 'I'. So happiness must be my true and essential nature. Happiness is not the nature of my body, which itself is an inert, experienced object. 'I' is the pure Consciousness, which illumines the inert body and makes it sentient. This pure Consciousness is all perfect and that is my true nature. It is not something outside. Whenever we experience happiness, in sleep or in pleasures, we always close our eyes. As we experience something beautiful, our eyes naturally close with happiness. Why? Because the experience of bliss and happiness is not something outside. It is deep within myself. A Man of Realisation lives with this awareness.

Nature of Desire

Once a desire arises, we cannot forget it. There is an insistence within to fulfill it, that things must happen the way we want. As long as we have such compulsive desires, it is impossible to gain peace. We cannot even sleep properly because our minds are so filled with desires.

Also once we have enjoyed something, we crave for it again and again. If we scratch, whence we feel itchy, we find that the itching increases. The nature of desire is the same. Once we start enjoying something, there arises more and more craving for it. Initially we desire pleasures we have not yet experienced and once we have enjoyed them, we keep remembering them and long to experience them again. When we sit for meditation or as we go to sleep, are these not the two things that disturb us - past experiences and future aspirations?

This does not mean that we should not plan for the future. It is not the day-to-day planning of work that we need to give up. The remembrance and desires for pleasurable experiences have to be given up.

My-ness Causes Sorrow

Besides desire, two other obstacles in attaining peace are the sense of 'I-ness' and 'my-ness'. The sense of 'I-ness' exists with reference to the body and its activities. When I feel I am this body, then I naturally feel that anything belonging to the body is mine. Thereafter, if I lose that object, I feel sad. The sorrow exists only because I have this 'my' sense. Suppose my watch is lost, will you be unhappy? No. But I will be! Suppose I give my watch to you, I no longer feel it belongs to me. Then if it is lost, it is okay. As long as there is the sense of 'my-ness', the mind is agitated. We feel sorrow only because of a sense of possession.

A businessman who had lost ten lakh rupees came to me once for advice. I told him, "The nature of business is such; sometimes there is profit, sometimes loss. You should have equanimity of mind in both profit and loss". He said, "Thank you, Swamiji. You have given me good advice". After a few days, he saw me unhappy. I told him that I had lost ten rupees. He said, "Swamiji, just a few days back when I had lost ten lakh rupees, you advised me to be calm. Now you are crying at the loss of only ten rupees!" I said, "My dear, the difference is that the ten lakh rupees were 'yours', but the ten rupees were 'mine'!"

'My-ness' causes suffering, whether the loss is big or small. The *Gītā* therefore says, 'He who is free from the sense of 'my-ness' attains peace'.

A teacher may say, "He is my disciple". Does this mean the teacher has a sense of 'my-ness' and therefore no peace? It is not so. It is only a practical use of the word 'my'.

How can we live in the world without a sense of 'my-ness'? It is not to be understood literally. Suppose someone asks me, "Swamiji, whose watch is this?" I cannot say, "I don't know" because the *Gītā* says, there should be no 'my-ness'. There is no harm in saying that it is mine, as long as I realise that the watch is merely in my keeping. All possessions are only in our temporary safe-keeping. What we must give up is the feeling of possession and our attachment to objects.

For example, when I travel by plane, I say, "My seat is number 25-A", but when I get off the plane, I do not try to take the seat with me! I accept it as mine only for the time allotted to travel. I relinquish it unhesitantly on completion of the journey. I do not really consider it as mine. We must live in the world and relate to people and objects in the same way. That is why mother, father, sister and brother are all called 'relatives' not 'absolutes'.

Ego Seperates

Now the question is, how can we give up I-ness (ahaṅkāra) or ego, which causes agitation and suffering? There is a simple exercise to reduce it. Its grosser manifestation is pride. All we need is a paper and pencil. We have this feeling that we are great – 'I did this, I achieved that'. Note down the names of all the people who helped us become what we are today.

Suppose I sing well. For me to be a good singer, how many people and things were necessary? I draw two columns on the paper and note down my contributions against the contributions of others. In weighing the two, my pride would disappear. In order to sing, I must be alive, and I have not created life. Again, I am gifted with a good voice, which is the Lord's gift. Next, I received training from my Guru and other musicians. And also I was tolerated by my family and neighbors who had to listen while I practised late at night!

How then can I have the pride that I sing well on my own merit? There is not a single thing that we can do or create on our own. Understanding this, our pride disappears. I then consider it as my privilege to serve and delight others. God has blessed me with this voice for that purpose. Abandoning any sense of doership, I become an instrument in the hands of the Lord.

The sense of 'my-ness' can be given up with the understanding that all that we have is a gift to us. Nothing is ours. We should love and care for all, but never with a sense of 'my-ness'. Thus, when desire, 'I-ness' and 'my-ness' leave, we will enjoy peace of mind.

Man does not gain peace by taking to drugs. Such a mind only gets shattered to pieces. He gains it by determining the nature of what is real, discovering and realising the Truth. It is 'the peace that passeth all understanding' – peace which is beyond our mind and intellect. Such peace never gets disturbed by anything. The *Gītā* says, "Having gained abidance in true peace even mountain-like sorrows do not disturb one".[1] That is the peace gained by the great. It is not achieved by running away from life. It is not the peace of a dullened mind or a mind in stupor. In such peace the mind is very much alive, awake, alert, vigilant, dynamically dealing with life and all its problems. It comes by the determination of the Reality. This approach of gaining peace and happiness is called the Path of Inquiry (Jñāna Yoga). There is another approach also – the Path of Devotion (Bhakti Yoga).

Path of Devotion

One who is devoted to the Lord and has faith that an almighty, omnipresent, omnipotent Lord is taking care of everything, has no reason to get agitated. Generally, we say that he who does not believe in the existence of God is an atheist. This is partially true. He who believes in the existence of God and still says, "I am worried and not peaceful", is also

---

[1] *yasmin sthito na duhkhena guruṇāpi vicālyate* – (6.22)

an atheist. He believes in the omniscience and omnipotence of the Lord and at the same time he is worried! What kind of belief is that?

If I have firm faith that the Lord is there to take care of everything, that He will give me the knowledge, strength and ability to do my work, then my duty is only to serve Him; I should have no agitations or worries and I am at peace. This is the Path of Devotion.

Path of Dharma

We can also attain peace of mind through the Path of Dharma (righteousness). When something that has to be done is not done or that which is not to be done is done, there is agitation. For example, if a child does not do his homework, he will be fearful of the teacher's wrath. If some work is left unfinished, we will always be disturbed by the thought, 'I have to do it'. Only when we do the work will we be at peace. Therefore, if one does all one's obligatory duties and stays away from prohibited actions, one is at peace. For one who follows the Path of Dharma, there is no fear and agitations.

By following any of the abovementioned means, man can attain peace. One may not have an inquiring or analytical intellect but has a simple faith that the Lord will take care of everything, he too will attain peace. Without faith, even day-to-day life becomes miserable. We see that distrust between spouses will cause agitations. Where there is faith, there is peace.

Peace is the true nature of the mind. Agitations are unnatural to the mind. That is why when the mind is agitated, we want to regain our natural state of peace. We ourselves are creating agitations, through desires, cravings, 'I-ness', 'my-ness', lack of faith and non-performance of our duties. When we remove these factors which cause agitations, we will have true peace of mind.

Proficiency and Efficiency

We are all fascinated with success. The inventor of the matchstick was very pleased with his invention, as it was a striking success! Every one wants success. What exactly do we mean by success? This analysis is important. Some are successful professionally, but is their life a success?

The general understanding of success is to attain a set goal or a desired result. A student who passes his exams, considers himself successful. We also hear of a 'successful' attempt on someone's life!

Three Factors of Success

Why does one succeed and another fail? Sometimes a person who has been successful many times fails miserably at some time.

Work: To succeed we need to work, even though we would love to succeed without work. There is only one place where success comes before work and that is in the dictionary! So work is a must for success.

Proficiency: Also we need knowledge – knowledge of the goal, the means to attain the goal and of our ability in reaching the goal. This knowledge is called proficiency.

Efficiency: We see that many people work tirelessly, laboriously and they have a lot of knowledge; still they do not seem to accomplish anything. This is because they lack efficiency. Efficiency is the third factor required for success. The skill or knack of performing an action so that it will bear the desired fruit is called efficiency.

In India more emphasis is given to theoretical knowledge. Indian universities impart a lot of information, but practical knowledge is overlooked, while in some countries more emphasis is given to the practical aspect and efficiency in work. Therefore, even though so many students are graduating from universities in India, they do not succeed. This is because India has neglected the practical aspect.

Success requires work. Work must be backed by knowledge. Knowledge must be efficiently applied to produce result.

Real Success

What is success? Is it success in a particular field? One psychiatrist, said to me, "Swamiji, most patients have benefited from my treatment, but I myself am troubled". A brigadier once told me, "I command my whole brigade, but I cannot say a word to my children!" People are successful in their particular fields but they do not feel happy and fulfilled in their life. True success means to be able to face all situations in life. There may be physical ailments, financial constraints or family problems. Some are experts in handling certain problems but get shattered in facing others. Some think of committing suicide when faced with little disappointments. Some are afraid of death and are terrified at the thought of facing life!

Also, every success should not to be glorified. A murderer's success is condemnable. We do not congratulate, award or celebrate the success of the evil and their evil deeds. A gangster, smuggler, black marketeer or killer may succeed, but we do not glorify his success. Activities like cheating are performed with hard work, alertness, proficiency and efficiency but such success is never glorified. Such work is always done on the sly and is always accompanied by fear in the heart.

What is the kind of success we want in life? Sometimes it appears that a person pursuing the noble path fails miserably and the corrupt man seems to prosper. Yet, the failure of the person following the path of virtue is glorified, never the success of an evil man! Failure on the righteous path is nobler than success on the path of evil.

In all national freedom movements, the initial attempts of freedom fighters have been suppressed by the powerful forces of the ruling government. It would appear that the freedom fighters were not succeeding, but what was the end result? The great epic *Rāmāyaṇa*, narrates how Rāvaṇa, the demon king of Laṅkā, kidnapped Sītājī, the beautiful wife of Śrī Rāma. As he was taking her away, the king of vultures, Jaṭāyu tried to save Sītājī, but died in the battle with the powerful Rāvaṇa. So, who succeeded? Rāvaṇa succeeded in his mission to kidnap Sītājī. Jaṭāyu failed to save her. Yet Rāvaṇa never succeeded in making Sītājī his and died on the battlefield at the hands of Śrī Rāma, whereas Jaṭāyu died with his head on the lap of Lord Śrī Rāma. Therefore, we learn that achievement of the ultimate goal is true success, even if we may be faced with short-term or immediate failure. Also success is that in which there is the unfoldment of the personality and purification of the mind. Success must bring joy, peace and happiness in one's life.

True success is not merely to attain name, fame and wealth but also lasting happiness. Happiness that does not end sorrow is not true happiness. There should be a sense of fulfilment that we have achieved all that is to be achieved, or that we have done all that was to be done (kṛtakṛtyatā).

We keep getting disturbed by small things in life. If somebody does not smile, we become miserable. If someone smiles, we worry about why he or she is smiling! If somebody does not invite us to a wedding, we are unhappy. Every small incident becomes a prestige issue. There is no peace at all. Nowadays there are many courses on management, such as 'Time Management', 'Managerial Effectiveness' or 'Effective Communication'. They deal with some aspect of success. As a result of attending such courses we may become more effective managers and may even get a promotion in our company, but they may not give true peace and happiness.

Therefore success cannot be defined only as achieving the desired result but as attaining lasting peace and happiness as a result of consistently following the path of virtue. One may fail in one's attempt, but that failure is nobler than success gained by following unrighteous ways.

True Strength

Lord Śrī Kṛṣṇa says, "I am the strength in the strong". He does not merely mean physical strength. He adds, "I am that strength which is devoid of desire and attachment".[1] Desire is for something

---

[1] *balaṁ balavatāṁ cāhaṁ kāmarāga-vivarjitam – Gītā 7.11*

we do not have and attachment is towards things or beings we already possess. This seems to contradict our experience. Usually, the more the desire and attachment we have, the more ambitious we are, the more vigorously and consentiously we work. We feel that without desire, we will not put forth diligent efforts and long hours of work. For many, attachment seems to be a driving force behind their efforts. It appears that without desires or attachments people tend to become lazy and lethargic.

However a little more thought will show us the falacy in our thinking. The nature of desire is such that it multiplies. One desire gives rise to many more. Also, when a desire is fulfilled, it leaves a craving for the same object. We wish to enjoy the thing again and again. In some cases we get addicted to the thing or become obsessed with the person. All desires cannot be fulfilled all the time, for desirers outnumber the availability of desired objects. There is only one vacancy in the company, for which 200 apply; 199 people will be disappointed. When a desire is not fulfilled, the result is disappointment, dejection, frustration and the like.

What happens when the desire is very intense and it is not fulfilled? Some get shattered, some become violent and some depressed. How can such a person be happy? Therefore, strength does not come from desire or attachment. True strength is gained by following the path of dharma or righteousness .

Dharma gives Strength

It is very difficult to translate or explain the full significance of the Sanskrit word 'dharma'. One of its meanings is to perform our obligatory duties towards our family and society. In order to perform one's duty and follow the path of righteousness, a great amount of strength is required. Most of our actions are prompted by likes and dislikes. What we like to do, we do. What we dislike, we don't do even if it is our duty and has to be done. It is difficult for most of us to put aside our likes and dislikes. We can truly walk the path of dharma only when we have no likes, dislikes and attachments. For example, we will have to give up our attachment to sleep in order to wake up at 4.00 a.m. When a person consistently wakes up early, his attachment to sleep vanishes and his mind becomes stronger.

We are very firm in resolving, but weak when it comes to putting our decisions or resolutions into practice. We say, "I will do it tomorrow", and 'tomorrow never comes'! True strength is to follow the path of dharma. There may be many oppositions, obstacles, difficulties and moments of testing. Only a man who is strong, will be able to pass through those trials. When the going gets tough, it is the tough who keep going. Likes, dislikes and attachments make man weak. When man becomes weak, he compromises and when he compromises, he becomes weaker. Finally, all his efficiency is gone. The man who follows the path of dharma consistently, becomes so powerful that the whole world bows down to him. Nobody can shake him. He can neither be tempted nor threatened. He gains authority, power, strength and fearlessness. This is called true success. This cannot be achieved overnight. It comes through long practice.

Love and Dedication

What is beauty in action? When one performs one's duty consistently without desire and attachment, then one becomes strong. But for most, the very idea of performing our duty is painful. People say that there is no beauty in doing one's duty. Duty becomes a burden. People become tired even before they go to work at 10:00 a.m. They love weekends and Monday is their worst day. They feel 'weakened' at the very thought of going back to work and wait for weekends.

How can we learn to see beauty in our duties? When we work with love, devotion and dedication there is beauty. Then the burden of duty disappears. It becomes a 'joy', not a 'job' to be done. When a woman works at the office, she considers it her duty. She works for a certain number of hours and leaves at the prescribed time. But when she is taking care of her child at home, she does not say that she will work for so many hours only or that she will take a breakfast break from 8 am to 9 am. She does not feel that she is performing a bounden duty because the love for her child is natural.

In India we have many holidays, especially in the schools and colleges. We always looked forward to holidays when we were studying. But I remember when I entered the āśrama we never had holidays, not even on a Sunday. In fact, if for some reason we had no class, we felt sad. This shows that we had love for studying Vedānta. Therefore, doing one's duty without the notion 'I am doing my duty' is the best. The *Gītā* says, 'Perform your duties, dedicating them to the Lord'. One must have an ideal, an altar of dedication. We must surrender our likes, dislikes, attachments, pettiness and ego at a higher altar and should perform our duties joyfully and carefully. The Lord works through us when we perform such dedicated actions. He gives us the necessary strength and accomplishes the work. Success is guaranteed.

When a person works with inspiration, he never gets tired or exhausted. When man works for himself, there is only the perspiration of labour without joy. When he works for a noble goal, he is inspired. When working for a noble goal, man derives tremendous strength from his chosen altar of dedication. The nobler the goal, the greater will be the strength he gains. This is the beauty of love and dedication. This brings efficiency in action and fulfilment in life.

One Inspires All

We learn from the past that some powerful people who devoted themselves to wrong ideals eventually destroyed themselves and many others. If the mind is not pure and the goal is not noble, the final result will be disastrous. On the other hand, we see saints and sages, great men and women dedicated to art, literature and science. The mere mention of their names, inspires people years after their departure. Institutions and large organisations flourish in their names. This is true efficiency.

A beautiful Sanskrit verse translates, 'He really lives, in whose living, countless people live'. What can one say about such great souls! Even their death becomes an inspiration. Death only destroys their physical body, but not their life and work. One who has fulfilled his life and has blessed and inspired many others alone can be called a truly successful person. He alone is truly proficient and efficient. Such success gives true happiness and true strength to face whatever challenges confront us. Such happiness truly ends all sorrows. Such a life is an inspiration to all.

I pray to the Lord that He may bless all of us with proficiency and efficiency – which will lead us to real success in life.

Om tat sat